BEWARE OF THE DOG

polymer clay:
- stone-look green
- stone-look red
- tan
- white
- dark brown
- stone-look brown
- stone-look blue
- yellow
- brown
- black

2 dark brown glass seed beads
balsa wood: one 1½"x¾"x¹⁄₁₆" plank, one ⅛"x1½"x¹⁄₁₆" stick
tacky craft glue
white acrylic paint, small flat paintbrush
black fine-point permanent marker
3½"x1" piece of wood do-dads™ fence
basic supplies (see inside the front cover)

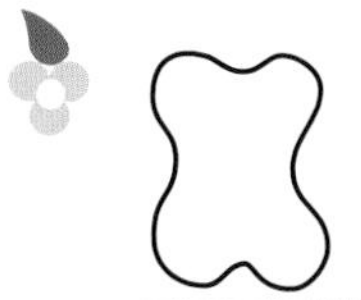

Before beginning, mix these colors:
Grass: a ¾" white ball with a 1¼" stone-look green ball
Dog: a 1¼" tan ball with a 1¼" stone-look brown ball
Spots: a ⅝" stone-look brown ball with a ⅝" brown ball
Flowers: a ¼" stone-look blue ball with a ⅛" white ball
     a ¼" stone-look red ball with a ⅛" white ball
     a ⅛" yellow ball with a ⅛" white ball
Nose: a ¼" brown ball with a ⅛" black ball

1 Sign: Use the knife to carve tiny pieces out of the sides of the plank. Paint both wood pieces white; let dry. Glue together as shown; let dry. Use the pen to outline the sign, write "BEWARE OF DOG" and draw a paw print. **Base:** Flatten a 1¾" grass ball into an ⅛" thick oval. Press a ⅜" grass-colored ball into the left end of the base. Press the sign into the mound. Press the fence into the back of the base. Press both pieces deep enough to stand independently, then gently remove them.

2 Legs: Roll four ¾" dog-colored balls into tapered logs. Press upward with your thumb at the wide end of the log to flatten. Press the four legs together. Use the knife to cut three toes in each leg. Press the legs gently onto the right front base. **Body:** Roll a 1⅛" dog-colored ball into an egg and press onto the top of the legs. **Head:** Roll a ⅞" dog-colored ball into a pear. Press onto the top front of the body.

3 Ears: Shape one ½" dog-colored ball and one ½" spot ball into teardrops. Indent one side of each with the rounded end of the paintbrush. Press onto the top back of the head. **Tail:** Roll a ⁵⁄₁₆" dog-colored ball into a ½" long tapered log. Press the wide end into the back of the body, curving the tail upward as if he were wagging it. **Eyes:** Press the seed beads into the middle of the face (see inside the back cover). **Nose:** Press a ³⁄₁₆" nose-colored ball under the eyes. **Face:** Use the pin to indent a vertical line under the nose, three dots on each cheek, two eyelashes and eyebrows.

4 Spots: Flatten several ⅛"–½" spot-colored balls. Press them to the body, legs, tail, ears and head. **Top knot:** Flatten a ⅛" spot-colored ball. Cut partially in half. Gently twist and press onto the top of the head, curving upward. **Flowers:** Place three ⅛" balls of the same color (pink mixture, blue mixture or white) together. Press the center with the rounded end of the paintbrush. Add a ⅛" ball of white to the center of each pink or blue flower and a yellow ball to the center of each white flower. Attach in clusters to the front and center of the base. **Leaves:** Flatten a ¼" grass-colored ball. Cut several ⅛" long grass-colored diamonds. Indent the center of each with the pin and press onto the sides of the flowers. **Bone:** Roll a ⁷⁄₁₆" white ball to ½" long log and flatten to ⅛" thick. Cut to ⅜" long. Separate and round the ends. Attach to the base near the flowers. Bake (see inside the back cover). After it has cooled, glue the fence and sign into their holes.

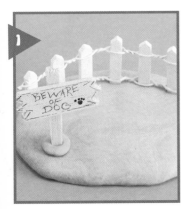

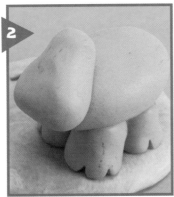

BUNNY IN A CROCK

polymer clay:
- stone-look brown
- red
- tan
- black
- white

$1\frac{5}{8}$" wide terra cotta pot
5" of 4-lb. monofilament nylon fishing line
four $\frac{3}{8}$" long black plastic whiskers
2 black glass seed beads
red/white checked fabric: one 2"x$\frac{7}{16}$" strip, one $\frac{9}{16}$"x$\frac{7}{16}$" piece
tweezers
tacky craft glue
basic supplies (see inside the front cover)

Before beginning, mix the following colors:
Body: a $1\frac{1}{4}$" stone-look brown ball with a $1\frac{1}{4}$" tan ball
Paws: a $\frac{3}{8}$" body ball with a $\frac{1}{4}$" white ball
Nose: a $\frac{1}{8}$" red ball with a $\frac{1}{16}$" white ball

1 Fill the pot to $\frac{1}{4}$" below the rim with a 1" ball of scrap clay. **Bunny body:** Shape a 1" body-colored ball into an egg. Press into the pot at an angle, with the small end toward the left back. **Feet:** Shape two $\frac{3}{4}$" body-colored balls into teardrops, then indent one side with your finger. Press them to the base of the body, inside the pot, with $\frac{2}{3}$ of the feet above the rim. Use the knife to cut two toe lines in the top of each foot.

2 **Arms:** Roll two $\frac{5}{8}$" body-colored balls into tapered logs. Round off the wide ends, then attach the small ends at the shoulders. Rest the arms along the pot rim with the paws beside the feet. Use the knife to add toe lines to each paw. **Head:** Shape a $\frac{7}{8}$" body-colored ball into a rounded triangle. Press onto the top of the body at an angle, so the bunny is looking to his right. **Ears:** Shape two $\frac{9}{16}$" body-colored balls into teardrops. Flatten to $\frac{1}{8}$". **Inner ears:** Roll two $\frac{3}{16}$" paw-colored balls to $\frac{1}{2}$" long and flatten. Press one onto the center of each ear. Use the pin to indent three times around the outside of each inner ear. Press the ears at the back of the head.

3 **Muzzle:** Flatten two $\frac{3}{16}$" paw-colored balls. Press side by side onto the lower half of the face. Use the pin to make three holes in each side. **Mouth:** Flatten a $\frac{1}{8}$" paw-colored ball and press it underneath the muzzle. **Nose:** Flatten a $\frac{3}{32}$" nose-colored ball and press it to the top of the muzzle. Use the pin to make three dots in each muzzle. **Eyes:** Press the seed beads above the muzzle (see inside the back cover). Use the pin to press eyelashes and eyebrows above the eyes. **Whiskers:** Cut six $\frac{3}{4}$" long pieces of fishing line. Use the tweezers to insert three into each side of the muzzle. **Paw pads:** Flatten six $\frac{1}{16}$" paw-colored balls. Press three to the top of each foot in a triangle. Roll two $\frac{1}{8}$" paw-colored balls into logs, then flatten. Press one under each paw triangle.

4 **Ladybug bodies:** Press a $\frac{3}{8}$" balls of red onto the table, flattening the bottom. Repeat with a $\frac{7}{16}$" ball. **Heads:** Press a $\frac{1}{4}$" black ball to the front of each body, making sure it touches the table. Use the pin to draw a line down each body as shown. **Spots:** Press two $\frac{3}{32}$" balls onto each ladybug. **Antennae:** Use the tweezers to push two black whiskers into the top of each head. Bake the bunny and bugs (see inside the back cover). Let cool completely. Glue the ladybugs to the pot as shown in the large photo. Glue the ends of the fabric strip together, then pinch in the middle to form a bow, glue to the bunny's left ear. Glue the two fabric rectangles between the ladybugs.

DEAR CASEY

polymer clay:
- stone-look blue
- stone-look red
- stone-look green
- white • black
- magenta • pale peach

3" long black wire
6" of white thread
two 2" lengths of ¼" wide dowel
pale peach acrylic paint

#4 flat paintbrush, pink chalk
blond Mini-Curl Curly Hair™
2" wide sinamay hat
2 black glass seed beads
½" wide silk daisy on a 1" long
   stem
clay cutters: ¾" heart , ⅜" star
tacky craft glue
basic supplies (see inside the
   front cover)

1 Shoes: Roll two ¾" white balls into ovals. Flatten four ¼" black balls to 1/16" thick and place one on each side of each shoe. **Socks:** Flatten two ⅜" white balls to ⅛" and press onto the top back of the shoes. **Legs:** Paint each dowel; let dry. Push one into the middle of each sock and down into the shoes. **Shorts:** Shape a 1¼" blue ball into a triangle. Slice ½" up from the center bottom; imprint a small "V" at the top of the split. Round the edges of the shorts. Gently insert the top of a leg into each short leg, keeping the shoes as close together as possible for added support. Gently flatten the bottoms of the shoes so she stands independently. Push ½" length of toothpick into the center top of the shorts, leaving ¼" exposed.

2 Arms: Roll two 11/16" magenta balls into tapered logs. Attach one to each shoulder. **Straps:** Roll two ⅜" blue balls into 3/16" thick logs and flatten. Place one over each shoulder. **Buttons:** Use the paintbrush handle to press a ⅛" white ball into the bottom of each strap. Use the pin to make two holes in each button. **Hands:** Attach a 7/16" pale peach ball to the end of each arm. Use the pin to make a small hole in each hand. **Head:** Press the center of a 1" pale peach ball onto the toothpick at the top of the body. **Eyes:** Press the seed beads into the middle of the face (see inside the back cover). Use the pin to add three eyelashes to each eye. **Cheeks:** Rub the paintbrush on the chalk, then use it to blush her cheeks.

3 Pocket: Flatten a ¼" blue ball to ⅛" thick. Cut into a ½" square and attach to the front of the overalls. Use the pin to make the stitches. **Patches:** Flatten a small magenta and stone-look red ball to 1/16" and cut each into ¼" squares. Press each onto the right leg of the overalls. Use the pin to make

indents around the edges of the patches as shown. **Pocket flower:** Flatten a stone-look red ball to ⅛" and use the star cutter to make a flower. Flatten a 1/32" white ball in the flower center, then press the flower onto the pocket. Use the pin to make stitches around the sides and bottom of the pocket. **Heart:** Flatten a stone-look red ball to ⅜" and use the heart cutter. Use the pin to make a hole through the bottom of the heart. **Flower:** Flatten five ⅛" magenta balls and place in a circle. Flatten one ⅛" white ball and place in the flower center. Shape two ⅛" green balls into teardrops and attach one on each side. Use the pin to indent the petals and leaves. Bake the girl, heart and flower separately (see inside the back cover). Let cool.

4 Hair: Cut fifteen 2" hair lengths. Spread glue over the top of her head and press one end of each length into it, starting at one side and moving around the head; let dry. Trim the hair and make bangs. **Hat:** Glue to the top of her head. Glue the front brim to the crown, then glue the clay flower to the same spot. Coil the wire around the paintbrush handle. Slip the end through the hole in the heart and bend down to secure. Glue into her right hand. Glue the silk flower into her left hand. Cut two 3" lengths of white thread and tie each into a shoestring bow. Glue one to each shoe where the black patches meet.

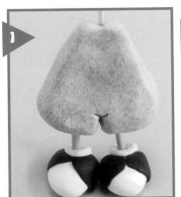

BARNYARD TANGLE

polymer clay:
- *white*
- *black*
- *white pearl*
- *pale peach*
- *ivory*
- *magenta*
- *yellow*

8 black glass seed beads
basic supplies (see inside the front cover)

1 **Cow—Body:** Roll a 1¼" white ball into an egg. Press the bottom flat. **Legs:** Roll four ¾" white balls into ⅝" long tapered logs. Indent the wide end of each with your thumb. Press the small ends into body as shown. **Head:** Roll a ⅞" white ball into a pear. Attach to the front of the body, making sure the chin touches the table.

2 **Ears:** Shape a ⅞" white ball into a teardrop; repeat with black. Press the small end onto the top back of the head, resting between the front legs and the face. **Horns:** Mix a ¼" black ball with a ⅛" white ball. Roll into a 1" long log and taper both ends. Press onto the top back of the head and curve the ends upward. **Tail:** Roll a ⅜" white ball to a ¾" log. Press one end to her rump and curl to one side.

3 **Spots:** Flatten six ⅛"–½" black balls to ⅛" and place one on each leg, one on the white ear and one on the right side of the cow's face. Use the knife to indent the top of each leg for a hoof. **Muzzle:** Shape a ⅜" pale peach ball into an oval and flatten to ¼". Press onto the front of the head. Flatten a 1/16" pale peach ball and place under the large one. Use the rounded end of the pin to imprint nostrils. **Eyes:** Press two seed beads into the middle of the face (see inside the back cover). Use the pin to draw two eyelashes and an eyebrow above each eye.

4 Pig—Legs: Roll four ⁹⁄₁₆" pale peach balls into ½" long tapered logs. Place the wide end of each foot on the back of the cow, pressing the legs together. Use the knife to indent each leg for a hoof. **Body:** Press the center of a 1" pale peach ball onto the top of the legs at a slight angle. **Head:** Shape a ¾" pale peach ball into a rounded triangle. Attach to the front of the body so the pig faces slightly left of the cow.

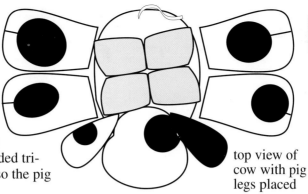

top view of cow with pig legs placed

5 Tail: Roll a ¼" pale peach ball into a ½" long rope. Press one to end to the pig's rump and twist into a coil. **Ears:** Flatten two ⅜" pale peach balls to ⅛"x½" diamonds. Press one to the right side of the head, facing forward. Press the other to the left side of the head, facing backward, then fold forward to give the pig an alert, interested look. **Snout:** Flatten a ¼" pale peach ball to ⅛" and press onto the bottom of the face. Flatten a ¹⁄₁₆" pale peach ball to ¹⁄₃₂" and press below it. Use the rounded end of the pin to poke nostrils in the muzzle and a mouth in the top of the ¹⁄₁₆" ball. **Eyes:** Press two beads into the middle of the face just above the muzzle. Use the pin to made two eyelashes and an eyebrow above each eye.

6 Sheep—Legs: Roll four ⁷⁄₁₆" pearl balls into ⅜" long tapered logs. Place the wide end of each foot on the pig's back, angling right as shown. Press the legs together. Use the knife to press a line in each foot for a hoof. **Body:** Roll a ⅞" pearl ball into an oval. Press onto the legs at the same angle. Use the rounded end of the pin to imprint curls all over the body for a woolly look. **Head:** Roll a ⁹⁄₁₆" pearl ball into a ½" long log. Flatten the sides into a diamond. Indent the front slightly with your finger. Press onto the front of the body, angling so it faces in the same direction as the cow. Use the knife to make a "Y" in the front for the nose and mouth.

7 Ears: Shape two ⅜" pearl balls into teardrops. Press onto the back of the head. **Eyes:** Press a bead into each side of the face. **Tail:** Flatten a ¼" pearl ball and press onto the rump of the sheep. **Bangs:** Flatten a ¼" pearl ball and press onto the top of the head, covering the ends of the ears. Use the pin to imprint wool all over the body, tail and bangs.

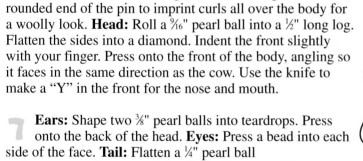

8 Chicken—Body: Shape a ¹¹⁄₁₆" ivory ball into a rounded triangle. Place on the sheep's back. **Wings:** Shape two ¼" ivory balls into triangles. Place one on each side of the body. Use the pin to indent feathers on the bottom of each wing. **Comb:** Roll a ¼" magenta ball to ¾" long. Press flat, attach to the top of the body and pinch the top edge to a point. **Beak:** Shape a ¹⁄₁₆" yellow ball into a cone and attach ¼" below the top of the body. **Eyes:** Press two beads into the body, just above the bead. Bake (see inside the back cover).

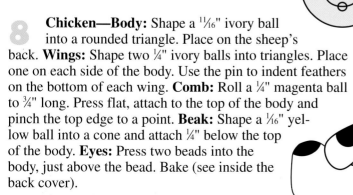

SNOW SCENE

polymer clay:
- *stone-look blue*
- *stone-look red*
- *stone-look turquoise*
- *white*
- *orange*

1½" high wood letters: S N O W
clear sparkle
white acrylic paint
snow texture paint
1" of 32-gauge fabric-covered wire
matte acrylic spray sealer
6 black glass seed beads
small flat paintbrush
pink chalk
basic supplies (see inside the front cover)

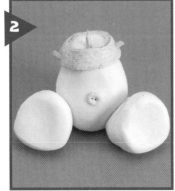

1 **Letters:** Paint the letters white; let dry. **Base:** Press a 2½" white ball out to 10"x2"x½". Curve forward as shown. Press the letters into the clay, making sure there is 2" empty at the left end, 1¾" at the right and ¾" at the back. Gently remove the letters. Bake the base (see inside the back cover); let cool. Glue the letters to the base. Set aside for step 9.

2 **Seated snowgirl—Body:** Shape a 1⅛" white ball into a pear. **Legs:** Shape two ¾" white balls into tapered logs. Use your thumb to indent on the wide end. Attach the other end to the body, extending forward so she is seated. **Scarf:** Flatten a 4" long stone-look red rope to ¹⁄₁₆" and cut a ⅜"x2" strip. Wrap around the top of the body, pressing the ends together in the back. Cut off the excess clay. Break a toothpick in half and insert one to half into each shoulder, leaving ¼" extending. Insert a toothpick into the top of the body, leaving ½" extending. **Button:** Roll a ⅛" stone-look red ball. Press onto the front of the body. Use the rounded end of the pin to indent. Use the pin point to add two holes in the center of the button.

3 **Arms:** Shape a ⁹⁄₁₆" white ball into a tapered log, rounding off the wide end. Press the small end onto an arm toothpick; repeat. Rest the arms on the legs as shown. **Head:** Shape a ⅞" white ball into a rounded triangle. Press gently onto the neck toothpick. **Hat:** Flatten a well-kneaded 1¼" stone-look red ball to ¹⁄₁₆" thick. Use the pattern to cut a triangle. Wrap the base around the head. Press the back edges together. Leave point upward until the brim is done. **Brim:** Roll a ¾" stone-look red ball to 4". Flatten to ³⁄₁₆" thick. Press around the base of the hat. Cut off excess and join in back. Pull the hat tip down and drape to one side. Mix a ½" stone-look red ball and a ⅜" white ball. Roll into three ⁷⁄₁₆" balls. Attach one for the hat pom pom. Slightly flatten one on each side of her head for earmuffs.

4 **Snowboy with hat—Legs:** Shape two ¾" white balls into tapered logs. Use your thumb to indent the wide end. Press the legs together and insert a toothpick into each, extending ½". **Body:** Shape a 1⅛" white ball into a pear. Press onto the leg toothpicks, centering so the figure stands balanced. **Scarf & Button:** Follow page 6, step 2 to make the scarf and button, but substitute stone-look turquoise for stone-look red. Insert the toothpicks as directed.

5 **Arms, Head, Hat & Earmuffs:** Follow page 6, step 3 to make the arms, head, hat and earmuffs, but substitute stone-look turquoise for stone-look red. Position as shown. **Snowball:** Place a ⁷⁄₁₆" white ball in the snowperson's left hand.

6 **Center snowboy—Legs and body:** Follow step 4 to make the legs and body. Follow page 6, step 3 to make the arms, letting them hang for now.

7 **Head:** Shape a ⅞" white ball into a rounded triangle. Press gently onto the neck toothpick. **Earmuffs:** Flatten two ⁷⁄₁₆" blue balls to ¼" thick and press one onto each side of the head. Press a small hole in the top of each for the wire.

8 **Faces—Nose:** Roll three ¹⁄₁₆" orange balls into ovals and press one into the middle of each face. **Eyes:** Use the pin to place two beads just above each nose (see inside the back cover). Use the pin to make six dots to form a smile and imprint three eyelashes on each eye. **Cheeks:** Rub the paintbrush on the chalk, then use it to blush their cheeks.

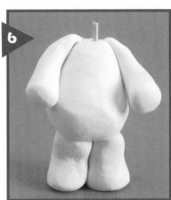

9 Place the snowpeople on the base as shown. Adjust the hands and other parts—the center snowman needs to have his hands lifted and placed on the "O". Carefully lift the figures from the base and place them on the baking sheet. **Snowball pile:** Stack three ⅜" white balls. Bake (see inside the back cover).

10 **Gluing:** Glue the snowpeople to the base and the snowballs to the top of the "S"; let dry. Glue the wire ends into the holes in the blue snowperson's earmuffs. Use the paintbrush and a toothpick to brush snow paint onto the base, letters, figures and snowballs. Be sure to create lots of peaks and valleys in the snow and use it to hide any awkward gaps between the base and the figures; let dry. Spray the entire pieces with matte spray; while the spray is still wet, sprinkle glitter over the piece. Let dry thoroughly.

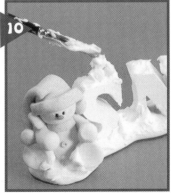

WOODLAND STACK

polymer clay:
- *brown*
- *white*
- *tan*
- *beige*
- *black*

6 black glass seed beads
small paintbrush (such as a small flat or liner brush)
basic supplies (see inside the front cover)

slightly thicker than the middle. Bend the small ends forward and press them onto the head behind the ears. Make two slices in each antler. Use the pin to make stitch marks around the edges of the antlers.

1 Moose—Body: Roll a 1¼" brown ball into an egg. Flatten on the work surface with the large end to the back. **Legs:** Roll four ¾" brown balls into tapered logs. Press the small end into the body as shown. **Head:** Roll a 1" brown ball into a pear. Press onto the front of the body, making sure the chin touches the table. Indent with your thumb, emphasizing the muzzle. Use the paintbrush handle to imprint nostrils at the top of the muzzle.

2 Ears: Shape two ⅜" brown balls into teardrops. Press the small end of each ear to the top back of the head so they rest between the front legs and the head. **Tail:** Roll a ¼" brown ball into a fat cone and place at the end of the body. **Antlers:** Shape two ½" beige balls into a teardrop. Gently flatten to ¼" thick, leaving the edges

3 Hooves: Flatten four ⅜" black balls to ⅛". Cut a slash in the top of each, then press one to the end of each foot. **Eyes:** Use the pin to insert two beads (see inside the back cover) into the moose's face, just above the muzzle. Use the pin to draw two eyelashes and an eyebrow above each eye.

4 Bear—Legs: Roll four ⅝" black balls into ⅝" long tapered logs. Insert ½ of a toothpick into the wide end of each. Push the toothpicks of two feet into the moose's back and two into the back of his head, pressing the legs together at the top for stability. Insert ½ of a toothpick into the top of each leg. **Body:** Press the center of a 1¼" black ball onto the leg toothpicks. Insert a ½ toothpick into the body front, extending ¼" in the direction the head will face. **Tail:** Attach one to end of a ¼" black ball to the bear's rump and twist into a teardrop.

5 **Head:** Slightly flatten a $^{13}/_{16}$" black ball. Push onto the toothpick to face slightly left of the moose. Use the rounded end of the pin to indent the head where the ears will go. **Ears:** Roll a $^3/_{16}$" black ball into a $^3/_4$" long log. Fold in half and pinch the ends together. Push the ends into an ear hole; repeat for the other ear. **Muzzle:** Shape a $^3/_8$" beige ball into a rounded triangle. Press onto the middle of the face. Use the pin to make a line halfway up from the center bottom. Press a $^1/_8$" beige ball onto the bottom of the muzzle.

6 **Nose:** Shape a $^1/_8$" black ball into a rounded triangle. Press onto the top of the muzzle, point down. Use the pin to imprint three whisker holes in each side of the muzzle. **Eyes:** Use the pin to insert two black beads (see inside the back cover) into the bear's face, just above the muzzle. **Claws:** Flatten a $^3/_8$" beige ball to $^1/_{16}$". Cut twelve $^1/_8$" triangles. Press three onto each foot as shown.

7 **Raccoon—Body:** Shape a $^{11}/_{16}$" tan ball into a pear. Insert a toothpick into the wide end and into the back of the bear. **Legs:** Roll two $^7/_{16}$" tan balls into tapered logs. Gently push upward on the wide end of each to form a foot. Press the small end onto the body, with the feet extending forward over the bear's back as shown. Use the pin to imprint two toe lines on top of each foot. **Arms:** Roll two $^3/_8$" tan balls into tapered logs and round the wide end. Press the arms to the shoulder with the paws resting on top of the feet. Use the pin to indent two toes lines in each.

8 **Head:** Shape a $^5/_8$" tan ball into a rounded triangle. Attach onto the top of the body. **Ears:** Shape two $^3/_{16}$" tan balls into flat triangles. Indent the centers and place one on each side of the head. **Mask:** Flatten two $^3/_{16}$" brown balls to $^1/_{16}$" and shape into triangles. Roll two $^3/_{32}$" white balls to the same length as the triangle sides. Attach one white piece to one side of each triangle. Attach to the face, white sides out and inner points touching. Use a pin to imprint fur lines along the outer edges. **Eyes:** Use the pin to press a bead into the inside bottom of each mask. **Muzzle:** Shape a $^1/_4$" white ball into a rounded triangle and press onto the middle of the face, under the mask. **Nose:** Press a $^1/_8$" black ball onto the top of the muzzle.

9 **Tail:** Roll a $^1/_4$" black ball, a $^1/_8$" and a $^1/_4$" tan ball, a $^1/_4$" brown ball and a $^1/_4$" white ball. Attach together as shown in the pattern; roll into a smoother log, taping the white end to a point. Use the pin to texture the tail. Press the tan end to the lower side of the raccoon and curve the tip over his shoulder.

Pads: Flatten six $^3/_{32}$" brown balls and place three on each foot in a triangle. Roll two $^1/_8$" brown balls into ovals and flatten. Attach one to the center of each foot as shown. **Belly:** Shape a $^3/_{16}$" white ball into an oval and flatten. Press onto the center of the belly. Bake (see inside the back cover).

side view of raccoon's foot

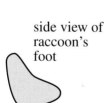

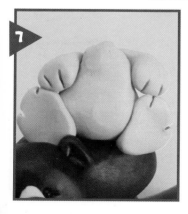

NATIVE AMERICAN COUPLE

polymer clay:
- *pale peach*
- *black*
- *beige*
- *brown*
- *turquoise*

4 black glass seed beads
pink chalk
small flat paintbrush
basic supplies (see inside the front cover)

Flesh: Before beginning, mix a 1¼" pale peach ball with a ½" brown ball.

1 **Boy—Legs:** Shape two ¾" beige balls into 1½" long tapered logs and place them side by side. Use the pin to draw a line along the side of each pant leg and fringe under it. **Tunic:** Shape a 1¼" beige ball into a cone. Press onto the top of the legs. Use the pin to make fringe at the bottom of the tunic. Imprint three X's down the front. **Moccasins:** Attach a ⅝" brown ball to each leg. Roll a ½" brown ball to 2½" long. Flatten to ⅛" thick. Wrap half around each leg above the moccasin. Cut any excess, joining the ends at the back of the leg. Use the pin to draw fringe around the cuffs and evenly spaced dots around the toes as shown.

2 **Arms:** Shape two ¹¹⁄₁₆" beige balls into tapered logs. Press one to each side of the tunic as shown, making sure there is ½" between the bottom of his left arm and the work surface. Use the pin to draw a pattern of X's and stitches along the outside of each arm. Insert a toothpick into the top of his shirt so ½" extends at the neck.

3 **Head:** Push a ⅞" flesh ball onto the toothpick. **Ears:** Press a ⅛" flesh ball onto each side of his head and use the pin to indent. **Mohawk:** Roll a ½" black ball to 1" long, then flatten the sides. Shape to the curve of the head, pinching the top to a point at each end. **Headband:** Roll a ⅜" beige ball to 2" long and press flat. Wrap around his forehead, joining in the back. Trim any excess clay. Press three ¹⁄₁₆" turquoise balls onto the front as shown.

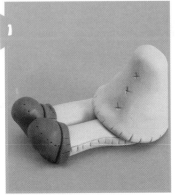
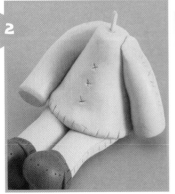
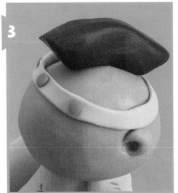

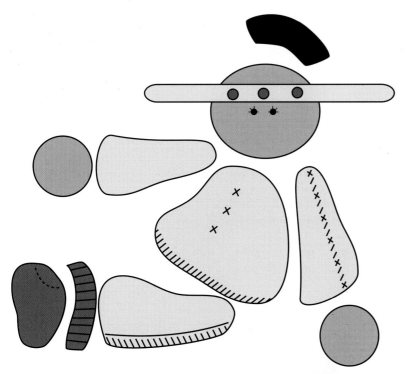

4 **Hands:** Attach a $7/16$" flesh ball to the end of each arm. **Eyes:** Press the seed beads into the middle of the face (see inside the back cover). Use the pin to draw the eyelashes.

5 **Girl—Legs:** Shape two $3/4$" flesh balls into $1\frac{1}{2}$" long tapered logs and place them side by side. **Dress:** Shape a $1\frac{1}{4}$" beige ball into a cone. Press onto the top of the legs. Use the pin to make fringe at the bottom of the tunic. **Moccasins:** Attach a $5/8$" brown ball to each leg. Roll a $1/2$" brown ball to $2\frac{1}{2}$" long. Flatten to $1/8$" thick. Wrap half around each leg above the moccasin. Cut any excess, joining the ends at the back of the leg. Use the pin to draw fringe around the cuffs and evenly spaced dots around the toes as shown. Insert a toothpick into the top of his shirt so $1/2$" extends at the neck.

6 **Arms:** Shape two $11/16$" beige balls into tapered logs. Press one to each side of the tunic as shown, making sure there is $1/2$" between the bottom of her right arm and the work surface. Use the pin to draw stitches along the outside of each arm. **Head:** Place a $7/8$" pale peach ball on her shoulders.

7 **Hair:** Flatten a $5/8$" black ball to $1/8$" thick. Press onto the head, starting in the back and wrapping to the front. Use the pin to draw the part. **Ponytails:** Shape two $9/16$" black balls into teardrops. Flatten the wide end of each. **Wraps:** Flatten two $1/4$" turquoise balls and use the pin to indent a hole in each. Push the small ends of the ponytails into the holes, then attach one to each side of the hair, draping them over her shoulders.

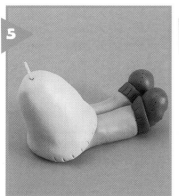

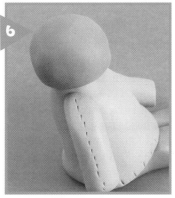

8 **Jewelry:** Flatten three $1/8$" turquoise balls and press them in a triangle to the front of her dress as shown. **Eyes:** Press the beads into the middle of the face (see inside the back cover). Use the pin to draw the eyelashes. **Hands:** Attach a $3/8$" pale peach ball to the end of each arm. Referring to the large photo on page 10, press the two figures together back to back, leaning the girl's head into the boy's back. Tuck their hands together, with the girl's under the boy's. **Cheeks:** Rub the paintbrush on the chalk, then use it to blush her cheeks. Bake (see inside the back cover).

TEDDY IN MY POCKET

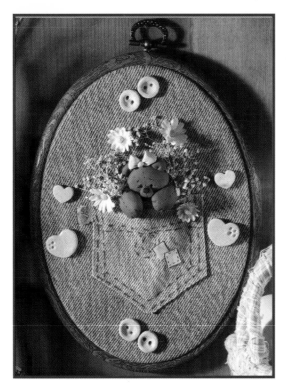

polymer clay:
- stone-look red
- stone-look blue
- brown

5½"x8" oval brown plastic woodgrain embroidery hoop
blue denim fabric: one 7"x10" piece, one 2¾" square
clay cutters: ½" and ¾" hearts, ½" circle
six 1"–2" sprigs of white dried baby's breath
four ½" wide white silk daisies
fine-point permanent marker: brown, black
low temperature glue gun and sticks
cotton balls
three ⅜"x½" fabric pieces: 2 pink, 1 blue
basic supplies (see inside the front cover)

1 **Pocket:** Insert the large denim piece into the embroidery hoop and tighten to hold securely. Follow the pattern to cut the pocket from the medium square. Use the marker to draw the stitches. Run a line of glue around three sides of the pocket, then center it on the denim in the hoop. Quickly insert cotton into the pocket and smooth the sides, leaving room to insert the bear. Let dry; remove the cotton.
Patches: Use the back pen to write "SS" on one pink patch and draw stitches around the white patch. Glue the "SS" patch to the top left of the pocket. Glue the remaining patches to the pocket as shown.

2 **Bear—Neck:** Roll a ¾" brown ball into a ¼"x1¾" log.
Head: Shape a ⅞" brown ball into a rounded triangle. Place onto the neck and slip into the pocket to adjust the length, if needed. The head should rest on the top edge of the pocket—no part of the neck should show. **Muzzle:** Shape a ¼" brown ball into a rounded triangle and attach onto the lower head. Use the pin to make stitch marks from the top of the head to the muzzle and down the muzzle.
Nose: Press a ⅛" black ball onto the top of the muzzle.
Eyes: Press the seed beads into the middle of the face (see inside the back cover), then use the pin to draw eyelashes and eyebrows.

3 **Arms:** Roll two ⅝" brown balls into tapered logs. Round off the wide end. Gently press the narrow end to the neck, just below the head. Arrange the arms forward and cup them over the pocket edge, resting against her muzzle as shown. Use the pin to draw stitch marks down each arm and imprint two toe marks on each paw.
Ears: Roll two ¼" brown balls into ½" logs. Fold the ends of each inward and press one on each side of her head. **Bow:** Shape two ¼" red balls into triangles. Press the points together and attach a ⅛" stone-look red ball to the center. Use the pin to indent fold lines. Attach onto the top of the head.
Patches: Flatten two 1/16" red balls into ¼" squares. Press one onto each elbow, then use the pin to draw stitches around the outside of each.

4 **Hearts & Buttons:** Flatten a ½" blue ball to ⅛" and a ½" red ball to ⅛". Cut two circles and a large and a small heart from each color. Use the pin to make four holes in one shoulder of each large heart. Indent the center of each button, then imprint two holes in the center of each. Bake (see inside the back cover). Glue the bear into the pocket. Glue the hearts, buttons and silk daisies to the denim as shown. Glue the baby's breath into the pocket with the shorter sprigs on the outside.

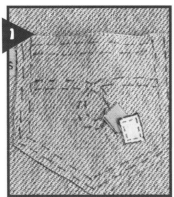

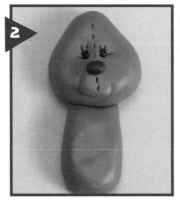

BOO PARTY

polymer clay:
- *white (or glow-in-the-dark)*
- *black*
- *orange*
- *yellow*
- *brown*
- *green*

acrylic paints: white, black
1½" tall wood letters: B O O
wood sealer, dark wood stain
paintbrushes: #4 flat, #1 liner
1½" of 24-gauge green wire
6 black glass seed beads
black construction paper
6" of heavy thread
sandpaper
soft cloth, tacky craft glue
orange chalk, small flat paintbrush
basic supplies (see inside the front cover)

1 Sand the letters, clean with the cloth and stain; let dry. Paint the front black; let dry. Use the liner brush and white paint to make stitch marks around the letters; let dry, then seal. Glue the letters together. Let dry. **Bodies:** Shape three ⅞" white balls into exaggerated teardrops. Arrange one so it is sitting on top of the middle "O". Arrange another leaning out from behind the "B", indenting him slightly around the letter to mark his position. Press the remaining body to the table, then curl the tail sharply upward. Set him in front of the last "O".

2 **Arms:** Roll six 5⁄16" white balls into tapered logs. Flatten two to ³⁄16" and attach to the back of the top ghost, as if he were leaning on them. Attach one to each side of the front ghost, extending outward, as if he is holding onto the "B" with one hand and balancing with the other. Flatten the last two and attach one to each side of the right figure, extending forward as if in welcome. **Heads:** Press a ⅞" white ball to the top of each figure. **Curls:** Roll three ¼" white balls into cones and press one to the top of each head, twisting into a curl.

Eyes: Press two beads into the middle of each ghost's face (see inside the back cover) and use the pin to draw eyelashes. **Cheeks:** Rub the paintbrush on the chalk, then use it to blush their cheeks. Gently take the ghost figures off the letters and place them on a baking sheet, being sure not to disturb their position.

3 **Pumpkin:** Flatten the bottom of a ⅞" orange ball and press it against the letters as shown in the large photo. Use the thread to imprint segment lines. Use the rounded end of the pin to poke a hole in the top. **Leaves:** Shape two ⅛" green balls into diamonds. Use the pin to draw vein lines. Lay on top of the pumpkin, extending to the sides. **Stem:** Roll a ¼" brown ball into a cone. Insert the tip into the holes and curve the top to the left.

4 **Candy corn:** Flatten a 5⁄16" orange ball, a 5⁄16" yellow ball and a ⅜" white ball to ⅛" thick. Layer as shown and cut into ⅛" wide slabs. Cut four triangles out of the slabs clay. **Bat:** Shape a ⅜" black ball into a rounded triangle. Cut a slice into each side for the wings. Shape two ⅛" black balls into triangles and press one onto each side of the top for ears. Press two eyes into the front. Attach a 1⁄32" orange ball for his nose. **Wire:** Wrap around the liner brush handle to create a spring. Press one to end into the bat and the other end into the top ghost's head; remove. Bake all the clay pieces (see inside the back cover). **Wings:** Cut two wings from construction paper. Glue one into each side of the bat. Glue the ghosts, pumpkins and candy corn onto the BOO as shown in the large photo. Glue one end of the wire into the bat and the other into the top ghost's head.

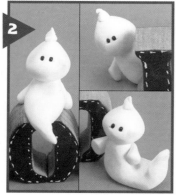

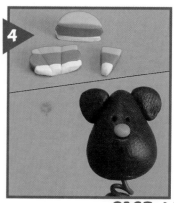

SCARECROW

polymer clay:
- *stone-look blue*
- *orange*
- *black*
- *brown*
- *beige*
- *tan*
- *stone-look brown*
- *yellow*
- *green*
- *burgundy*
- *white*

one 6" strip of straw-colored fringed thin felt
6" of heavy thread
tacky craft glue
4 black glass seed beads
basic supplies (see inside the front cover)

Before beginning, mix the following mixtures:
Light blue: a ⁷⁄₁₆" blue ball with a ⁷⁄₁₆" white ball
Light brown: a 1" brown ball with a ⅝" tan ball

1 **Pumpkins:** Follow page 13, step 3 to make seven pumpkins, but begin with four ¾"–⅞" and three ½"–⅝" orange balls. Make only one leaf for each pumpkin. Cluster the pumpkins as shown.

2 **Scarecrow—Pants:** Roll two ¾" stone-look blue balls into 2" tapered logs. **Cuffs:** Flatten two ⁷⁄₁₆" light balls to ⅛". Press one onto the bottom of each leg. **Feet:** Shape two ½" brown balls into ovals and press one onto the bottom of each cuff. Set side by side on top of the ¾" pumpkin and bend into a sitting position. Use the pin to imprint folds and gathers so the legs look natural. **Leg patches:** Flatten ⅛" balls of burgundy, orange and yellow to ¹⁄₁₆". Cut each into a ¼" square. Attach as shown. Use the pin to indent two or three stitches around each patch.

3 **Shirt:** Shape a 1¼" burgundy ball into a cone. Press your thumb against the bottom back to slightly indent it. Attach the wide end to the tops of the legs, letting some hang over the backs. **Arms:** Roll two ⅝" burgundy balls into 1¾" long tapered logs. Attach at the shoulders, then bend to rest on the knees. Use the pin to imprint folds at the elbows as shown. **Hands:** Press a ½" white ball into the end of each arm. Slightly flatten and rest on the knees. **Arm patches:** Flatten a ⅛" ball each of orange and yellow. Cut each into a ¼" square. Attach one to each elbow and use the pin to indent two or three stitches around each. **Buttons:** Use the rounded end of the pin to press two ⅛" yellow balls into the shirt front. Use the pin point to add two holes in each button.

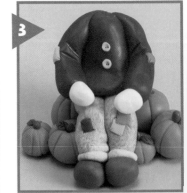

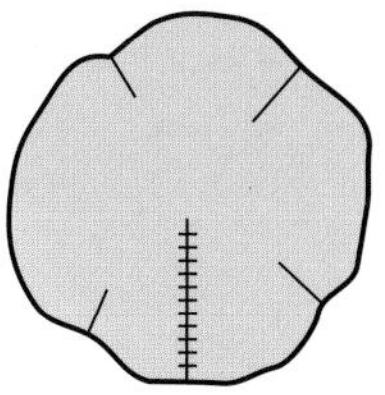

4 **Collar:** Flatten a ⁹⁄₁₆" beige ball to ⅞" wide. Gently ruffle the edges. Use the pin to indent the sides every ½". **Head:** Break a toothpick in half and insert into the collar with ¼" extending up. Push the center of a ⅞" beige ball onto it. Imprint a line up the front center of the collar and over the top of the head, then add horizontal stitch marks to the line. **Nose:** Flatten a ⅛" burgundy ball to ¹⁄₁₆" and cut a ⅛" tall triangle. Attach to the center of the face. **Eyes:** Use the pin to insert a bead on each side of the vertical line, above the nose. Use the pin to draw an eyelash and eyebrows above each eye. **Features:** Use the pin to draw a crooked mouth below the nose, then add cross marks.

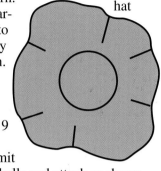

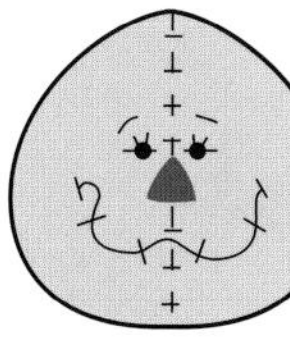

collar

5 **Hat brim:** Flatten a ⅞" light brown ball to 1¾" wide. Use the pin to indent the sides as shown on the pattern. Press onto the top of the head curving it around the head and flaring the edges. **Crown:** Flatten a ½" light brown ball and attach to the brim center. **Hat patches:** Flatten a ⅛" ball each of burgundy and yellow; cut each in a ¼" square. Press onto the hat as shown. Use the pin to indent two or three stitches around the sides of each patch.

hat

6 **Crow:** Follow page 5, step 9 to make a chicken, but use black for the body and wings; omit the comb. Flatten two ¹⁄₁₆" black balls and attach as shown for a top knot. Press onto the left pumpkin. Bake (see inside the back cover). **Straw:** Clip the fringe from the fabric to make many ⅜" lengths. Apply glue to the ends of the strands and use a toothpick to insert them into the crevices at the ankles, wrists, collar and under the hat as shown in the large photo on page 14.

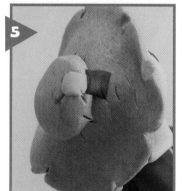

NORTHWOODS SANTA (CONTINUED FROM PAGE 16)

3 **Pocket:** Flatten a ¼" red ball to ¹⁄₁₆". Cut out a ¼" square for a pocket and attach onto the upper left shirt. Use the pin to make stitches around three sides of the pocket. **Patches:** Flatten two ¼" green balls to ¹⁄₁₆". Cut out two ¼" squares and attach one near each elbow at an angle. Use the pin to add stitches at two corners. **Shirt details:** Use the pin to imprint two lines a ¼" apart down the shirt front. Use the rounded end of the pin to attach three ⅛" black balls between the lines. **Head:** Push a 1" pale peach ball onto the neck toothpick. Be sure the figure is still balanced.

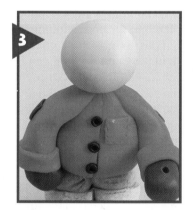

4 **Beard:** Shape a ¾" white ball into a log. Taper at both ends and wrap around the chin as shown. **Hair:** Flatten a ⅜" white ball into an oval and press onto the back of the head, covering the bare space between the beard ends. **Ears:** Press a ³⁄₁₆" pale peach ball to each side of the head and use the pin to indent. **Sideburns:** Roll two ¼" white ball to ¾" long, flatten and wrap one above each ear in an arc. **Cheeks:** Flatten two ⅛" pink balls and place ¼" apart ¼" above the beard. **Mouth:** Press a ⅛" pink ball above the center of the beard. Use the rounded end of the pin to indent. **Mustache:** Shape two ⅜" white balls into flat teardrops. Attach as shown, curving the tips toward the sideburns. **Nose:** Press a ¼" pale peach ball into the top of the mustache. **Eyes:** Use the pin to insert two beads (see inside the back cover) above the nose. Draw two eyelashes outside each eye. **Eyebrows:** Shape two ⅛" white balls into teardrops and flatten. Place one above each eye. **Tuft:** Roll a ³⁄₁₆" white ball into a cone and press one to end to the top of the head, twisting to curl. Bake (see inside the back cover). Use the black pen to draw the plaid pattern onto the shirt and patches as shown. Spray with sealer and glue the fern sprig into his left hand.

NORTHWOODS SANTA

polymer clay:

- *tan*
- *translucent*
- *white*
- *green*
- *black*
- *yellow*
- *stone-look blue*
- *red*
- *pale peach*

2 black glass seed beads
one ½" sprig of green preserved tree fern
fine-point black permanent pen
matte acrylic spray sealer
pink chalk, small flat paintbrush
basic supplies (see inside the front cover)

Before beginning, mix the following mixtures:
Gold: a 1" tan ball with a ¾" yellow ball
Light blue: a ½" white ball with a ½" stone-look blue ball
Pink: a ⅛" red ball with a ¼" white ball

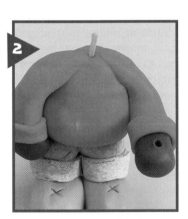

1 **Soles:** Shape two ⁹⁄₁₆" translucent balls into ovals and flatten to ¼". Use the pin to indent the sides of the soles every ¼" to create the look of waffle soles. **Boots:** Shape two ¾" gold balls into ovals and press onto the soles. Attach them side by side. **Legs:** Shape two ⅝" stone-look blue balls into 1" long tapered logs. Place the wide end of one on top of each boot, pressing the sides together. Insert a toothpick into the middle of each leg, leaving ¼" sticking out at the top to support the body. **Cuffs:** Roll light blue into a 4" log and flatten to ¹⁄₁₆". Cut into a ⅜" strip. Start at the center back and wrap around the bottoms of the pants. Trim off any extra clay. Use the pin to press in the center front as shown and to draw an "X" in the front top of each boot.

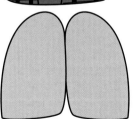

2 **Shirt:** Shape a 1¾" red ball into a pear. Center it over the legs and push down on the toothpicks. Adjust so the figure stands upright. Insert a toothpick into the top center of the shirt, leaving ¼" extending to attach the head. **Arms:** Roll two ¾" red balls into tapered logs. Attach one on each side of the body, with the small ends at the shoulders. His right arm hangs down his side and the left arm extending forward. **Hands:** Shape two ½" green balls into ovals and attach one at the end of each arm. **Cuffs:** Roll a ½" red ball into a 2" long log and flatten. Cut two ¼"x2" strips. Attach one around the bottom of each arm. Use the pin to poke a hole in the top of his left hand.

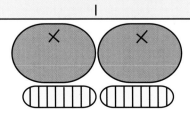

left arm
(side
view)

Directions continued on page 15.